Sailing through China

Sailing through China

PAUL THEROUX

Illustrated by
PATRICK PROCKTOR

HOUGHTON MIFFLIN COMPANY

BOSTON

1984

First American edition 1984

Text copyright © 1983 by Paul Theroux
Illustrations copyright © 1983 by Patrick Procktor

Library of Congress Cataloging in Publication Data

Theroux, Paul.
Sailing through China.

1. Yangtze River Valley (China) – Description, and
travel. 2. Theroux, Paul. I. Procktor, Patrick.
II. Title.
DS793.Y3T48   1984   915.1'2045   83–12575
ISBN 0–395–34836–6; (limited) 0–395–35492–7

Designed by Humphrey Stone

Set in Palatino
Printed and bound in Great Britain

00 10 9 8 7 6 5 4 3 2 1

There is no Yangtze River. The name is unknown to most Chinese, who call it Ta Jian, 'Great River', or Chang Jiang, 'Long River', unless they live above Chungking – there, the swift silt-filled waters are referred to as Chin-sha Jiang, 'The River of Gold Sand'. That is only a misnomer now. As recently as fifty years ago, in the winter months when the level dropped, the Chinese squatted at its edge and panned for gold, sluicing the mud and gathering gold dust. European travellers reported seeing washerwomen wearing thick gold bangles, made of the metal that had been carried from where the river – let us call it the Yangtze – rises in Tibet.

But it has more moods than names. 'I am careful to give the date of each day's notes,' Archibald Little wrote in *Through the Yangtse Gorges* (1887). 'The river varies so wonderfully at different seasons that any description must be carefully understood only to apply to the day upon which it is written.' Captain Little was overwhelmed by it; he compared it to the Mississippi and the Amazon; he said it was indescribable. It has in many stretches a violent magnificence. It is subject to murderous floods, and its winter level creates rapids of such turbulence that the river captain steers his ship through the foam and travels down the tongue of the rapid, praying that no junk will lie in its path, as it is impossible for him to stop or reverse. But it is not all so dramatic. Its four divisions are like four separate rivers: above Chungking, it is mythic and still associated with gold and landslides; the Upper River (Chungking–Yichang) is the wildest – here are the gorges and the landscape of China's Walter Scottish classic, *The Romance of the Three Kingdoms*; the Middle River (Yichang–Wuhan) is serene and a mile wide; the Lower River (Wuhan–Shanghai) is slow and sticky yellow and populous.

I sailed 1,500 miles downstream, from Chungking to Shanghai. Every mile of it was different; but there were 1,200 miles I did not see. It crosses ten provinces, 700 rivers are joined to it – all Yangtze statistics are hopelessly huge and ungraspable; they obscure rather than clarify. And since words can have a greater precision than numbers, one day I asked a Chinese ship captain if he thought the river had a distinct personality.

He said, 'The mood of the river changes according to the season. It changes every day. It is not easy. Navigating the river is always a struggle against nature. And there is only one way to pilot a ship well.' He explained – he was smiling and blowing smoke out of his nostrils – 'It is necessary to see the river as an enemy.'

Later, a man told me that in the course of one afternoon he had counted nine human corpses bobbing hideously down the river.

The Yangtze is China's main artery, its major water-way, the source of many of its myths, the scene of much of its history. On its banks are some of its greatest cities. It is the fountainhead of superstition; it provides income and food to half the population. It is <u>one of the most dangerous rivers in the world</u>, in some places one of the dirtiest, in others one of the most spectacular. The Chinese drink it and bathe in it and wash clothes in it and shit in it. It represents both life and death. It is a wellspring, a sewer and a tomb; depthless in the gorges, puddle-shallow at its rapids. The Chinese say if you haven't been up the Great River, you haven't been anywhere.

They also say that in the winter, on the river, the days are so dark that when the sun comes out the dogs bark at it. Chungking was dark at nine in the morning, when I took the rattling tin tram on the cog railway that leads down the black crags which are Chungking's ramparts, down the sooty cliffs, past the tenements and billboards ('Flying Pigeon Bicycles', 'Seagull Watches', 'Parrot Accordions') to the landing stage. A thick sulphurous fog lay over the city, a Coketown of six million. The fog had muffled the morning noises and given the city an air of frightening solemnity. It also stank like poison. Doctor Ringrose, who was from Leeds, sniffed and said, 'That is the smell of my childhood.'

There were <u>thirty-three of us,</u> including Ringrose. The others were American, most of them millionaires, many of them multi-millionaires. 'If you have two or three million,' one of them told me in the dreary city of Wanxian, 'you're not a millionaire – you're just getting by.' Another enlarged on this. Not to be a poor

7

millionaire you needed twenty-five million. 'If you have twenty-five,' she said crisply, 'you're all right.' But Lurabelle Laughlin, from Pasadena, had inherited 50 million dollars. Her husband Harry told me this. He said Lurabelle could buy and sell every person on board our ship. He wasn't being malicious, only factual. 'And I'm not too badly off myself,' he said.

'I hate walking,' Mrs Ver Bryck told me. Mrs Ver Bryck, another oil heiress, hailed from Incline, Nevada. 'I never walk. I've been everywhere and didn't have to walk. I pay so I don't have to walk. And stairs are my bugbear. But you look like a walker, Paul. Are you going to walk and do all that crappy-ola?'

I cherish the memory of Ami Ver Bryck and Lurabelle Laughlin walking from the tramway at Chungking across the muddy paving on the foreshore, with hundreds of Chinese in baggy blue suits, watching in utter silence. Lurabelle's mink coat was golden, made from thirty-five creatures of the 'tourmaline' variety; Ami's was a rich glossy mahogany. And here was Bea Brantman, also in mink. 'This is my football coat,' she cried. 'I wear it to all the games.' Bea and her husband, who was known to everyone as Big Bob, had eleven children. Big Bob said, 'I guess they'd put me in jail for that in China! Watch out, Bea, it's kind of slippery here. It looks more like an ocean than a river. You can't even see the other side.'

It was a good companionable crowd, and though it seems a contradiction to say so, these millionaires represented a cross-section of American society. Some had inherited their money, some had got it from divorce settlements, or had married into it, or had made it from nothing. One had made it from brokering, another from gun accessories, another from burglar alarms, four were oil fortunes, one was advertising, others didn't say. Some struck me as rather stupid, with their cowboy novels and their remarks about building condominiums near Hankow or Yichang and all the talk about Connecticut. Some were very smart about Chinese history or porcelain and talked intelligently about why they disliked Norman Mailer, and they knew the various dates in the Cultural Revolution. They were Democrats and Republicans, Jewish and Christian, they came from all over the United States. Interestingly, they never argued among themselves, no one was ever on the outs, and the spouses never fought. All of them had travelled before. Half had already been to China once and knew their way around Inner Mongolia. The rest were novices and called Mao 'Mayo', and confused Thailand with Taiwan, and Fuji with Fiji. They were as tenacious and practical as the Chinese, and just as ethnocentric, but much funnier, and better at cards.

We boarded *Tung Fang Hong* ('The East is Red') *Number 39* and were soon under way. Because of the construction of locks and a dam at Yichang, we would travel down river in two ships: the M.S. *Kun Lun* awaited us just below Yichang. Both *Number 39* and the *Kun Lun* were the same size, built to carry 900 people. But they had been specially chartered by the Lindblad Tour Company. There were, as I say, only thirty-three of us, and a crew of 102. No hardships for us, and it seemed at times, though we were travelling through the very heart of the country, that China was elsewhere.

My mind kept going back to my first impression of China, and my disbelief. We had left the frenzy, the scavengers, the free-for-all of Hong Kong and were heading towards the hills – so blurred and blue you might mistake them for clouds. China began there, on those bare hillsides. There were voices behind me.

'Look, Jack.'

'Yeah.'

'Lush vegetation.'

But for an hour, until the train reached the Chinese border at Lo Wu, it was not lush. It was still farming country, dusty fields and skinny crops, as far as my eye could see.

Mrs Ver Bryck was saying to me, 'I've been every-where, more than once.' I took her to be well over seventy. In fact, she was just sixty-two. She chain-smoked. She had a shopping bag full of cartons of cigarettes. In another shopping bag she kept her supply of vodka. On this Express to Canton, she told me how much she liked the Chinese. She loathed Italians – they controlled all the gambling in Nevada, she said. She despised the Japanese – they had charged her $410 for a room in Tokyo a few days before. It was the Royal Suite, but she had not asked for it, and she had spent only twelve hours in it. That was $34 an hour. She looked out the window at the cabbages, the lettuce, the beans, and at the culverts and ditches. 'Look how they work,' she said. 'I love the Chinese.'

Just before Lo Wu there was a fence – coils of barbed wire about twenty feet high – and then, as the train penetrated The People's Republic of China, billboards by the side of the trains advertising 'Ginseng Bee Secretion' and 'Tiensin Shoes and Slippers' and 'Marlboro Cigarettes'. And inside the train, on a television set that had been showing a Chinese travelogue about Kweilin, there were commercials for 'Rainbow Brand' television sets and 'Ricoh' watches – men and women dancing sedately and all of them wearing Ricoh watches. It was all a flatter, duller version of Hong Kong commercialism, this communist parody of advertising; and it was a bit sad, because it was the imperfect mimicry of the Hong Kong vulgarity which was in turn an imitation of American crassness. It was saddest of all because it was unconvincing.

And it bore no relation at all to what was going on outside the train window. There in Kwantung Province everyone was harvesting rice. The train tracks were surrounded by paddy fields. Some of the rice was already tied into bunches, and the rest was being gathered by hand or threshed. They threshed it the old way, by whipping the rice grains into a basket. The people worked in groups, never alone. In one field, about eighty people were working in the heat, and this was the beginning of my disbelief. It was rural; I did not want to think how primitive this method was.

The land looked scraped – no trees, only tiny houses, or huts, and cultivation everywhere. In places there were small stands of scrub pine or tall weedy eucalyptus trees.

But there was no shade. The people working in the dazzling dust had black cloth fringes sewn to their coolie hats to keep off the sun. Some were yoked to huge watering cans, and they looked like miniature crucifixions in the mass of these bald hills.

That was the other strange thing: it was not lush. It was hot, even tropical, but the hills were naked, bald, scarred with plough-marks and paths. I saw an old man whipping a buffalo's wrinkled back with a stick to beat him out of a ditch.

The first town, an hour out of Lo Wu, was a railway junction named Tang t'ou-hsia. Outside it was a brickworks. Men and women were making bricks in the old way here, out of mud and straw, clumping them out of brick moulds and stacking them into a cathedral shape which they turned into a furnace. Sweltering, the brick-bakers stoked the fire. All the houses in this area were made of these liver-coloured bricks.

'What do you think?' Mrs Ver Bryck asked.

'Rustic,' I said. 'Very nice.'

But it was mournfully backward: no cars, no tractors, no threshing machines, no metal – only farming by hand, and brickmaking. I saw no livestock – no pigs, no chickens. It was like all the pictures I had seen of old China: the same baggy smocks and sandals and straw hats, the same laborious agriculture, the same simplicity.

On the television set in the train a film of singing soldiers began to roll. They were well-dressed soldiers and as they sang a pretty girl in a red dress skipped through fields and past a waterfall. Outside the train,

13

people were harvesting rice, sweating their guts out in the brickworks; and there were soldiers there, too, standing by the tracks in their flimsy uniforms, looking too small to be soldiers, and wearing baggy pants.

Later, I could tell how important a person was by the way his blue suit fitted him.

The 'Blue Danube' was playing on the ship's loudspeakers as *Number 39* swung between the sampans and the fishing smacks and the burdened ferries. The captain greeted us in the lounge and told us the current was moving at two metres per second and added, 'As your captain, I am responsible for your safety, so please don't worry about it.'

Captain Liu was sixty. He had a narrow, flat-backed head and bristly hair and a seeping wound in his left eye and large spaces between his teeth. He had always worked on the river. His father had been a tracker on a junk, rowing and towing junks upstream. Captain Liu himself had started out as a steward, serving food on a Chinese riverboat, at the age of fifteen. 'I was the "boy" as they say in English, but I worked my way up to captain. I never went to school. You can't learn about this river in a school. You can only learn it by being on the bridge.'

This is true; and not much has been written about the Yangtze. But before I left London I had been given a list of twenty-eight landmarks on the Upper River, patiently typed by Captain A. R. Williamson, who spent nearly thirty years sailing up and down the river. Captain Williamson is ninety, living in vigorous retirement in Hove, and is one of the historians of the river. I was lucky in meeting him and lucky to have a detailed list of things to look out for – towns, cliffs, pagodas, rapids and shrines. It was Captain Williamson's list that convinced me that, though a great deal has changed in China ('China,' Premier Deng has promised, 'will be a modern power by the year 2000'), little on the Yangtze has altered. The cities are bigger and filthier, the rapids have been dynamited, there are more ships; but the river today is essentially the river Captain Williamson travelled on in 1920, and Archibald Little sailed on in 1886, and the Abbé David botanized on in the 1860s, and Italian missionaries proselytized on in the seventeenth and eighteenth centuries. The river and the ways of many of the river dwellers are as old as China. There is a painting in the Shanghai Museum of junks and sampans on a river, by Zhang Zheduan. Those vessels have the same sails, mats, rigging, rudders and oars as ones I saw on the Yangtze the other day. But it is a Sung Dynasty painting, 1,000 years old.

A half hour below Chungking, Captain Williamson's notes said, was a large Buddha in a shrine at the top of a long flight of steps. The niche was there, and the steps; but the Buddha was gone. In Captain Williamson's day, all upbound junks fired strings of firecrackers on passing the Buddha, 'in gratitude for safe passage'. Veneration has become political in China: there were no firecrackers, though there were dozens of passing junks.

Mottled hills appeared in the mist on both sides of the river, and here, just above Chang Shou, the river narrowed to about seventy-five feet. The ship slowed to negotiate this rocky bottleneck and gave me time to study the hills, Abbé David saw fortifications on the tops of these hills. In his *Diaries* is a wonderful account of his Yangtze trip. He wrote, 'These are refuges in times of trouble for the country people, where they can go with their possessions and be safe from the depredations of rebels and brigands.' Banditry was widespread on the Yangtze from the earliest times, and the 1920s and '30s were especially terrible, as warlords' armies fought their way towards Chungking; there was no peace on the river until 1949, when a brooding bureaucracy with parrot slogans took over.

Now, every inch of these hills was farmland: it is the agricultural overstrain of China. On the steepest slopes were terraces of vegetables. How was it possible to water the gardens on these cliff-faces? I looked closely and saw a man climbing up the hillside, carrying two buckets on a yoke. He tipped them into a ditch and, without pausing further, started down the hill. No one is idle on the Yangtze. In the loneliest bends of the river are solitary men breaking rocks and smashing them into gravel. You might think they would sit down and rest (who is watching?), or soak their feet in the shallows. It is killing work. But they go on hammering, and the sound I associate with these hidden stretches of the Upper River is the sound of hammers and chisels, a sound like the sweetest chimes.

In 1937 Captain Williamson saw only the city walls of Chang Shou from the river. Today there are no city walls, and Chang Shou (the name means 'Long Life') is one of the nightmare cities of the river. It burst through its old walls and sprawled across the banks, blackening three hillsides with chimneys and factories and blocks of workers' flats. 'Looks like Pittsburgh,' someone said. But Chungking had looked like Pittsburgh, and so did six others downstream. Yellow froth streamed from pipes and posterns, and drained into the river with white muck and oil and the suds of treated sewage and beautifully coloured poison. And on a bluff below the town, there was an old untroubled pagoda, still symmetrical, looking as if it had been carved from a piece of laundry soap.

These pagodas have a purpose. They are always found near towns and cities and, even now in unspiritual China, serve a spiritual function, controlling the *Feng-shui* ('Wind-water') of a place: they balance the female influences of the *Yin* ('Darkness') and the male influence of the *Yang* ('Light'). The Chinese say they no longer believe in such superstitious malarkey, but the visible fact is that most pagodas survived the Cultural Revolution. Anything that a fanatical Red Guard left intact must be regarded as worthy, if not sacred. The pagodas on the Yangtze bluffs remain pretty much as they always were.

It was near Chang Shou, about noon on that first day, that I saw a sailing junk being steered to the bank, and the sail struck, and five men leaping onto the shore with tow-lines around their waists. They ran ahead, then jerked like dogs on a leash, and immediately began towing the junk against the current. These are trackers. They are mentioned by the earliest travellers on the Yangtze. They strain, leaning forward, and almost imperceptibly the sixty-foot junk begins to move upstream. There is no level towpath. The trackers are rock-climbers: they scamper from boulder to boulder, moving higher until the boulders give out, and then dropping down, pulling and climbing until there is a reach on the river where the junk can sail again. The only difference – but it is a fairly large one – between trackers long-ago and trackers today is that they are no longer whipped. 'Often our men have to climb or jump like monkeys,' wrote a Yangtze traveller, in the middle of the last century, of his trackers, 'and their backs are lashed by the two chiefs, to urge them to work at critical moments. This new spectacle at first revolts and angers us, but when we see that the men do not complain about the lashings we realize that it is the custom of the country, justified by the exceptional difficulties along the route.' Captain Little saw a tracker chief strip his clothes off, jump into the river, then roll himself in sand until he looked half-human, like a gritty ape; then he did a demon dance, and howled, and whipped the trackers, who – scared out of their wits – willingly pulled a junk off a sandbank.

The trackers sing or chant. There are garbled versions of what they say. Some travellers have them grunting and groaning, others are more specific and report the trackers yelling, 'Chor! Chor!' – slang for 'Shang-chia' or 'Put your shoulder to it'. I asked a boatman what the trackers were chanting. He said that they cried out 'Hai tzo! Hai tzo!' over and over again, which means 'Number! Number'' in Szechuanese, and is uttered by trackers and oarsmen alike.

'When we institute the Four Modernizations,' he added – this man was one of the miniscule number who are members of the Chinese Communist party – 'there will be no more junks or trackers.'

One day I was standing at the ship's rail with Big Bob. We saw some trackers, six of them, pulling a junk. The men skipped from rock to rock, they climbed, they hauled the lines attached to the junk, and they struggled along the steep rocky towpath. They were barefoot.

Brantman winced. It was a wince of sagacity, of

understanding: Yes, it said, I now see what this is all about. Then he spoke, still wincing a little.

'The profound cultural differences between people!'

I looked at him. He was nodding at the trackers scampering among the rocks on the shore.

'They don't care about television,' he said.

I said, 'That's true.'

'Huh?' He was encouraged. He was smiling now. He said, 'I mean, they couldn't care less if the Rams are playing tomorrow.'

The Los Angeles Rams were Big Bob's favourite football team.

'Am I right, or not?'

'You're right, Bob,' I said. 'They don't care about television or the Rams.'

The junks and these trackers will be on the river for some time to come. Stare for five minutes at any point on the Yangtze and you will see a junk, sailing upstream with its ragged, ribbed sail; or being towed by yelling, tethered men; or slipping downstream with a skinny man clinging to its rudder. There are many new-fangled ships and boats on the river, but I should say that the Yangtze is a river of junks and sampans, fuelled by human sweat. Still, there is nothing lovelier than a junk with a following wind (the wind blows upstream, from east to west – a piece of great meteorological luck and a shaper of Chinese history), sailing so well that the clumsy vessel looks as light as a waterbird paddling and foraging in the muddy current.

That image is welcome, because there is little birdlife

on the Yangtze – indeed, <u>China itself is no place for an ornithologist</u>. It is hard to say if the absence of trees is the reason for the scarceness of birds; or is it the use of powerful insecticides, or the plain hunger of the people who seem to kill anything that moves? Apart from a few kites and hawks, and some feeble sparrows, the only wild ground-dwelling creature I saw in China was a rat, and in twenty-two trips on the Yangtze a Lindblad guide told me he had only seen one wild thing, a small snake. No wonder the Chinese stared at mink coats and alligator handbags! Abbé David saw very few birds on the Yangtze in the 1860s and, as a naturalist, he was looking hard for them. He put it down to the wilful destruction of animals by the Chinese, and his reflection on this has proved to be prophetic: 'A selfish and blind preoccupation with material interests has caused us to reduce this cosmos, so marvellous to him with eyes to see it, to a hard matter-of-fact place. Soon the horse and the pig on the one hand and wheat and potatoes on the other will replace hundreds of thousands of animals and plants given us by God.'

Down the Yangtze the awful prediction has been fulfilled. You expect this river trip to be an experience of the past – and it is. But it is also <u>a glimpse of the future.</u> In a hundred years or so, under a cold uncolonized moon, what we call the civilized world will all look like China, muddy and senile and old-fangled: no trees, no birds, and shortages of fuel and metal and meat; but plenty of pushcarts, cobblestones, ditch-diggers, and wooden inventions. Nine hundred million farmers splashing through puddles and the rest of the population growing weak and blind working the crashing looms in black factories.

Forget rocket-ships, super-technology, moving sidewalks and all the rubbishy hope in science fiction. No one will ever go to Mars and live. A religion has evolved from the belief that we have a future in outer space; but it is a half-baked religion – it is a little like Mormonism or the Cargo Cult. Our future is this mildly poisoned earth and its smoky air. We are in for hunger and hard work, the highest stage of poverty – no starvation, but crudeness everywhere, clumsy art, simple language, bad books, brutal laws, plain vegetables, and clothes of one colour. It will be damp and dull, like this. It will be monochrome and crowded – how could it be different? There will be no star wars or galactic empires and no more money to waste on the loony nationalism in space programmes. Our grandchildren will probably live in a version of China. On the dark brown banks of the Yangtze the future has already arrived.

It struck me that many of the American passengers were sedentary types. One man said to me, 'Back home, my wife and I lead a very sedimentary life.' I knew what he meant. And this was a kind of sedentary travel. Nor did these armchair travellers read books. They didn't talk about books – they talked about places. Many of their sentences began, 'When we were in Kenya . . .' Or it might be Tierra del Fuego or Inner Mongolia: they were well-travelled. For facts they seldom referred to books, or their reading, but nearly always to their travel. They had seen crime in Korea, or an election in Costa Rica, or poverty in Turkey. To me they said, 'You've got a big race problem.' It wasn't personal; they meant England – I lived there.

Most of them had discovered that if you had enough money and time you did not have to read. You could discover things for yourself – or, rather, be told about them by a National Guide. In the corporate lives that they led they had become used to people telling them things, filling them in on a situation. In China we had 'briefings'. They loved 'briefings'. You sat there and someone with a briefcase gave you the low-down – facts, figures, a little history – and you interrogated him for ten minutes. Then it was over. It was so much easier than reading, so much more reassuring. But, of course, as travellers we were regarded as big and busy; in a sense the commune workers and the people in factories and the sailors on the Yangtze ships were working for us.

One of us was not busy. She was an armchair traveller who spent all her time seated, usually soaking herself in whisky.

'I've known a lot of women like her,' a man told me. 'A hell of a lot of women. I've met them on trips like this. They go to Mongolia. They go to Pago-Pago. Peru. Sri Lanka. And they never do anything. We had one with us on the Galapagos trip. She never got off the ship! Can you imagine going to the Galapagos and not getting off the ship? It was a twenty-eight day trip!'

'Why do you suppose she came here?' I asked.

'To drink. Haven't you seen her? She's having a grand time. She's got a whole box full of whisky sours. She stays in the hotel and drinks while we're at the communes. The only thing is – she's got to drink them warm. She doesn't trust the ice. It's got germs in it – that's what she thinks. When it melts, the germs swim into her whisky sour.'

Later, he said, 'I'll make a prediction. I'll bet you she never gets off the boat on the Yangtze. She'll just sit there, drinking her whisky sours.'

He was right. But sometimes I was grateful for this old woman's company – at night, in the lounge of the *Tung Fang Hong – Number 39*, after everyone had gone to bed. By half past nine nearly everyone was in bed, except this woman and me, drinking and playing gin rummy.

One night she looked across the table and said, 'I was rotten spoiled,' and she smiled. 'My daughter was rotten spoiled. And I'm going to make goddam sure that my granddaughter is rotten spoiled.'

Sixty-five miles below Chungking, at Fooling, I was joined at the rail by one of the passengers, a stockbroker. We talked about the price of gold and the delinquent bullion market as, on the shore, small tent camps of Chinese sifted gravel and lugged it in buckets to waiting sampans. We passed gardens and talked about land deals and Washington real estate.

'Timber,' he said. 'This is a very good time to buy timber. Something like Weyerhauser. The slump in building has meant the stock's depressed. But you can't go wrong with timber. What you want is a well-managed company, with a good product and a good record.'

There was a commune on the next hill: vegetables, a factory, chimney, huts, a brickworks. We watched it pass. He told me the American stock market was vastly underrated. Then the dinner gong rang.

We were soon at Feng Tu. Abbé David: 'Very pretty because of its pagodas, towers and the green hills around it.' Captain Williamson: 'One hill is said to be haunted.' Nothing had been torn down, but a certain amount had been added: it was a sullen agglomeration of scorched factories and workers' flats under a weeping corona of smog.

'It certainly looks haunted to me,' I said to the Political Commissar on our ship. The Political Commissar is the labour relations man. If there is slackness in the galley or the engine room on a Chinese ship, the Political Commissar reminds the workers of their duties. Ours was Comrade Sun; he had been working on the river since 1950 ('just after Liberation'), when he was seventeen. He knew the hills and temples of Feng Tu very well.

No, he said, it was not haunted.

'There are no ghosts,' says a Chinese pamphlet entitled *Stories about Not Being Afraid of Ghosts*. 'Belief in ghosts is a backward idea, a superstition and a sign of cowardice. This is a matter of common sense today among the people. But while there are no demons . . . there are many things which resemble them – imperialism, reactionaries, difficulties and obstacles in work, for example.' Comrade Sun was a member of the Party: he agreed with this pamphlet.

We talked about river superstitions. It was not easy. He

did not want to give me the idea that people today were silly enough to believe any of this stuff. But I pestered him for frights and beliefs.

'There was an old belief,' he said, 'that if a fish jumped out of the water onto the deck of a ship you could not eat it. Fish often jumped onto the junks. They still do, when they're swimming upstream. Such fish were regarded as demons.'

'Did they throw the fish back?' I asked.

'No. They had to take it ashore. Dig a hole. Then bury it.'

'What do they do now?'

'Eat them.'

I had read of another belief of the junk sailors, that when the wind died they stood on the deck and whistled, to call the wind, so that they would not have to go ashore and tow the boat. Whistling up a wind may once have been a practice among old British sailors – the idea occurs in *Macbeth*. It struck me as a weird and attractive superstition.

Comrade Sun said yes, long ago it was believed that if you whistled the wind would rise. Then he smiled. 'I don't think it does any good at all.'

That evening, our ship, *Number 39*, anchored below the remote town of Shibao Block (Shih Pao Chai, or 'Precious Stone Castle'). This is one of the most unusual – and probably least spoiled – places in China. It is a perfect butte, a hundred feet high, which once had a monastery on top and now has a bare temple. The way to the top is up a staircase in an eleven-storey red pavilion built against the perpendicular side of the rock. Amazingly, it remains just as it was described by travellers a hundred years ago, and the view from the top is a reminder that there are towns in China with no factories, little mechanization, and only the oldest methods of ploughing and planting. The town at the base of the rock is a labyrinth of slimy alleys and muddy streets, and cobblestone passageways that look like the wynds of Edinburgh. And shops: carpenters, bakers, weavers of funeral wreaths, fruitsellers. Just outside the town an old man led a blindfolded buffalo trampling around in circles, to soften the mud for the making of bricks and roof tiles.

I had brought a snapshot to Shibao Block. It was one of Captain Williamson's and it showed the town through the simple eye of a box camera in 1927. The townsfolk were interested. They called the mayor, Comrade Lu, and examined the snapshot. They found it very odd. It was clearly their town, and yet one house was not where it should be. This snapshot was the past: they had never seen an old picture of the town. The mayor asked to be photographed holding the picture.

'Please take his picture,' the interpreter said. 'He is a big potato.'

He meant it as the highest praise.

Nearly the whole town of Shibao Block saw us off: silent faces staring at Howard Buhse's red golfer's cap and Ira Weinstein's foot-long telephoto lens and Lurabelle's mink and Jerry McCarthy's whirring cine camera and old

Mr Chase's tape-recorder (he recorded everything, even the sound of the ship's engines) and the pinks and blues of the ladies' $350 synthetic 'ultra-suede' dresses and my yellow suede shoes. We were bizarre. There was not a sound, not a murmur from the hundreds of people on the shore.

There were more watchers downstream at Wanxian, a city more nightmarish than Chungking – mud, rain, black streets, broken windows, smoke, and every housefront wearing a film of soot. It was once a city of great beauty, and famous for its perfectly poised *Feng-shui*. But the bluffs and hills that were praised are now covered with factories, the most shocking a silk filiature plant, where 1,300 women and girls were losing their health in the dim light, making silk thread from soaked cocoons. It was a sweat shop, all these women sacrificed to the manufacture of hideously patterned bolts of silk in garish colours. They worked quickly, silently, with ruined hands, to the racket of the jolting looms.

In the days that followed, we passed through the gorges. Many people come to the Yangtze for the gorges alone: they excite themselves on these marvels and skip the rest of the river. The gorges are wonderful, and it is almost impossible to exaggerate their splendour; but the river is long and complicated, and much greater than its gorges, just as the Thames is more than what lies between Westminster and Greenwich.

The great gorges lie below Bai De ('White King City'), the lesser gorges just above Yichang. Bai De was as poisonous-looking as any of the other cities, but as soon as we left it the mountains rose – enormous limestone cliffs on each side of the river. There is no shore: the sheer cliffs plunge straight into the water. They were formed at the dawn of the world, when the vast inland sea in western China began to drain east and wear the mountains away. But limestone is a curious substance. It occurs in blocks, it has cracks and corners; and so the flow zigzagged, controlled by the stone, and made right angles in the river. Looking ahead through the gorges you see no exit, only the end of what looks like a blind canyon.

FROM CAPTAIN WILLIAMSON'S NOTES

Pa Yang Hsia (Eight Cliffs Gorge): *About twelve miles below Wanhsien, the river flows through plateaux of sandstone for about five miles. On the left bank, three Buddhas are carved in the cliff-face and when the river falls low enough the little figures are cleaned and repainted.*

Yun Yang Hsien: *This city is on the left bank about 145 miles above Ichang. Opposite the city is a picturesque temple which is said to contain a magic bell.*

Bai De (White King City): *Below this important city the scene changes dramatically, as the river hence to Ichang – 110 miles – winds its way through gorges in the mountainous regions which lie athwart its course.*

Feng Hsiang Hsia (Wind Box Gorge): *Below Bai De is one of the most picturesque of the gorges, four miles long, precipitous sides, 700–800 feet in places. At the upper entrance to this gorge, off the left bank, is the isolated Goose Tail Rock – the summit about 80–90 feet above the river at winter level. Below the Goose Tail, the square holes of 'Meng Liang's Ladder' can be seen zigzagging up the right hand cliffs, on the right bank, while further down the gorge, in a niche high up on the left-bank cliffs, can be seen the ends of the 'wind boxes'.*

Wu Shan Hsien: *Below the Wind Box Gorge is an open ten-mile reach . . . end of the reach is Wu Shan Hsien, the easternmost city in Szechuan – a picturesque, romantic city, with its walls and drum towers – situated immediately above the entrance to the longest gorge of the river.*

Wu Shan Hsia (Wu's Mountain Gorge): *Wu (witch) was a legendary wizard who dwelt on the mountain at the first reach of this gorge and is credited with blowing a twenty-five-mile gap through the mountains to permit the river to pass.*

Kuei Chou (now called Zi Gui): *Picturesque small town on the left bank behind low prongs of projecting reefs.*

Niu Kan Ma Fei Hsia (Ox Liver and Horse Lung Gorge): *Situated below Kuei Chou, this gorge is four miles long on a bend in the river. It takes its name from a rocky outcrop on the cliff face on the left bank.*

Teng Ying Hsia (Lampshine Gorge): *This gorge is about eight miles long. At the end of the gorge the river turns abruptly left, into the Yellow Cat Gorge.*

Huang Mao Hsia (Yellow Cat Gorge): *In the bend is a large smooth round rock which, because of its appearance, is called*

The Sleeping Pig. This last of the gorges is about eight miles long, and at its lower end the river emerges into open country and reaches the port of Ichang.

After seeing the great gorges of the Upper Yangtze it is easy to believe in gods and demons and giants.

There are *graffiti* on the gorges. Some are political ('Mankind Unite to Smash Capitalism'), some are poetic ('Bamboos, flowers and rain purify the traveller'), while other scribbled characters give the gorge's name or its history, or they indicate a notable feature in the gorge. 'Wind Box Gorge' is labelled on the limestone, and the wind-boxes have painted captions. 'Meng-liang's Ladder', it says, at the appropriate place. These are the zigzag holes that Captain Williamson mentioned in his notes; and they have a curious history. In the second century A.D. the Shu army was encamped on the heights of the gorge. The Hupeh general, Meng-liang, had set out to conquer this army, but they were faced with this vertical gorge wall, over 700 feet high. Meng-liang had his men cut the ladder-holes in the stone, all the way to the top of the gorge, and his army ascended this way, and they surprised the enemy camp and overwhelmed them, ending the domination of Shu. (In 1887 Archibald Little wrote, 'The days are long past since the now effeminate Chinese were capable of such exertions . . .')

The wind blows fiercely through the gorges, as it does in New York between skyscrapers; and it is a good thing, too, because the junks can sail upstream – there is little room here for trackers. On the day I passed through, the sky was leaden, and the wind was tearing the clouds to pieces, and the river itself was yellow-brown or viscous and black, a kind of eel-colour. It is not only the height of the gorges, but the narrowness of the river – less than a hundred yards in places – which makes it swift, sixty metres per second in the narrower places. The scale gives it this look of strangeness, and fills it with an atmosphere of ominous splendour – the majestic cliffs, the thousand-foot gorge walls, the dagger-like pinnacles, and the dark foaming river below, and the skinny boatmen on their vessels of splinters and rags.

Archibald Little wrote, 'I rejoiced that it had been my good fortune to visit the Yangtse Gorges before the coming stream of European tourists, with the inevitable introduction of Western innovation in their train, should have destroyed all their old world charm.' The cities, certainly, are black and horrific, but the gorges are changeless and completely unlike anything I had ever seen before. In other landscapes I have had a sense of deterioration – the Grand Canyon looks as if it is wearing away and being sluiced, stone by orange stone, down the Colorado River. But the gorges look powerful and permanent, and make every person and artefact look puny. They will be here long after Man has destroyed himself with bombs.

It is said that every rock and cliff has a name. 'The Seated Woman and the Pouncing Lion', 'The Fairy Princess', and – less lyrically – 'The Ox-Liver and Horse-Lung Gorge' (the organs are boulder-formations, high on the cliff-face). The Yangtze is a river of precise nomenclature. Only simple, wild places, like the volcanic hills of south-west Uganda, are full of nameless topography; naming is one of the features of Chinese civilization and settlement. I asked the pilot of our ship if it was so that every rock in the Yangtze had a name. He said yes.

'What is the name of that one?' I asked quickly, pointing out of the window.

'That is Pearl Number Three. Over there is Pearl Number Two. We shall be coming to Pearl Number One in a few minutes.' He had not hesitated. And what was interesting was that these rocks looked rather insignificant to me.

One of the millionaires said, 'These gorges come up to expectations. Very few things do. The Taj Mahal did. The Pyramids didn't. But these gorges!'

We passed Wushan. There was a funeral procession making its way through the empty streets, beating drums and gongs, and at the front of the procession three people in white shrouds – white is the Chinese colour of mourning – and others carrying round paper wreaths, like archery targets. And now we were in the longest gorge, twenty-five miles of cliffs and peaks, and beneath them rain-spattered junks battling the current.

At one time, this part of the Yangtze was filled with rapids. Captain Williamson's list of landmarks noted all of them. They were still in the river, breaking ships apart, in 1937. But the worst have been dynamited away. The most notorious was the Hsin Lung Tan, a low-level rapid caused by a terrific landslide in 1896. It was wild water, eighty feet wide, but blasting opened it to 400 feet, and deepened it. Thirty years ago, only the smallest boats could travel on the river during the winter months; now it is navigable by even the largest throughout the year.

Our ship drew in below Yellow Cat Gorge, at a place called Dou Shan Tuo ('Steep Hill Village'). We walked to the road and took a bus to the top of the hill. Looking across the river at the pinnacles called 'The Three Daggers', and at the sun pouring honey into the deep cliffs, one of the passengers said with gusto, 'What a place for a condominium!'

The M.S. *Kun Lun* is by any standards a luxurious ship. She is popularly known as 'Mao's yacht' because in the 1950s and early '60s she was used to take visiting dignitaries up and down the Yangtze. Any number of prominent Albanians can boast that they slept in one of the *Kun Lun*'s sumptuously carpeted suites and danced in the lounge or got stewed to the gills in the sixty-foot-wide club room. The idea for the fancy ship was Jiang Qing's – Chairman Mao's third wife and now the celebrated political criminal of the Gang of Four. She had the guts of a river ship torn out and she redecorated it in the style of Waldorf Astoria Ming – art deco and lotus blossoms – and did not stint on the curtains or the blue bathtubs. The Gregorys (Fred and Merial) had a rat in their room, but never mind – Raymond Barre of France once slept in their suite.

The chief feature of this wilderness of antimacassars is space: wide passageways, large cabins, huge lounges, and sofas on which seven can sit comfortably and catch up on the *Peking Review* or listen to 'News About Britain' or 'The Book Programme' on the World Service of the BBC – there are two gigantic 'Spring Thunder' brand shortwave radios on board. You hardly notice the grand piano, the bar is so big. For this reason, the *Kun Lun* was 'criticized' during the Cultural Revolution; she was turned over to the people and more or less raped. Cots and bunks were crammed into the suites, and for four years the proletariat used her as an ordinary river ship. When the Lindblads found her a few years ago she was in mothballs. Mr Lindblad made a deal with the China Travel Service: he would fix her up, restore her to her original splendour if he was allowed to use her for tours. The scheme was agreed upon, and now the *Kun Lun* is afloat once again, as great an anachronism, as large a contradiction, as could possibly be found in the People's Republic.

We transferred from *Number 39* to the *Kun Lun*. We were on the Middle River now, and there were no complaints. Or rather, not many. I did hear a shrill drunken voice moan one evening, 'I hate Chinese food. Once a month, maybe. Not more than that. But every damned day? I can't eat the stuff.'

And another night, Mrs Ver Bryck looked at me tipsily and said, unprovoked and unbidden, 'Of course I'm happier than you are. I've got more money.'

We stayed two days at Wuhan. The river had become wider, the banks lower and flatter; but the cities had grown more interesting. We watched a thyroidectomy at a hospital at Wuchang, the patient anaesthetized by four acupuncture needles in her hands, and a little voltage; and in the early morning I prowled the streets of Hankow and noted that free markets had sprung up – until this year such improvisatory capitalism was forbidden. At six o'clock one morning I saw my first Chinese beggar, and on the next corner a trio of child acrobats balancing plates on their heads and doing handstands, and then passing the hat. New Hankow looked something like old Hankow.

At night in Hankow and Canton and other hot places where the windows were open I could hear people playing Mah Jong, the sounds of the tiles clicking like castanets and the chatter of the players. It has not been outlawed, and the various types of Chinese chess – *xiang qi*, which has certain similarities to our own chess game, and *wei qi*, which is the same as the Japanese game *go* – are actually encouraged. In alleys, sitting on overturned crates, Chinese men can often be seen playing cards, the game they call 'Aiming High'. In Hankow and Wuhan I saw gamblers throwing dice in the shadows, playing dominoes, and arguing over cards.

The suggestion that the Chinese might be gambling was always sharply denied. Gambling is seen as one of the worst things that a person could do, and there was such shock expressed when the subject came up that I was certain the urge to gamble was still strong.

'Games should be played just for fun,' Comrade Wu said. And he told me the story of the man who gambles away his money, his food, his radio, and is finally forced to use his wife to give value to a wager – and he loses the bet and his wife.

But there are all sorts of stakes. In Shanghai four men were squatting in an alleyway, playing cards. There was a bottle of home-made gin and pile of clothes-pins near the men. Each time someone lost a hand of cards he had to put a clothes-pin on his ear and take a swig of gin. The drunkest of them had a cluster of clothes-pins on his ear, and looked a complete jackass, which was of course the point – the others were laughing at him.

Public humiliation was a sort of teaching technique. A gambler paid his debt by submitting to humiliation. But if the gamblers were caught by the authorities they would be punished with another form of humiliation.

I had asked Comrade Wu what happened to people who were found gambling.

'Oh, it is very bad,' he said. 'They pay a fine, some are even put into prison. We *educate* them!'

'Educate' is said with force. It is discipline, a humiliation, and I seldom heard the word 'education' in China without its sounding like a hard smack in the face.

At Suchow primary school the headmistress said that they never used corporal punishment. They 'educated' people who used corporal punishment, 'and if a teacher cannot learn to teach patiently, and resorts to hitting, he is criticized.'

She made 'criticized' sound like a whipping. It was another form of discipline, a refinement of humiliation. A person, one of the billion, was criticized by being singled out and exposed. He was severely questioned by the various members of his block or commune and made publicly to show his contrition.

This, in effect, was what the Gang of Four trial was all about: it was public humiliation. The trial was its own punishment – it did not need any sentences at the end. Dragging someone out of a mob, singling out an individual, demanding that a student stand up while the others remain seated – these are the worst things that can happen to someone who values his anonymity and sees himself as part of the powerful Chinese army of workers. Isolated, the person loses his power and is humiliated and weakened by the gaze of the mob. In the nineteenth century it was done with the 'cangue' – those wooden collars that thieves were made to wear.

It is hard to disentangle education from discipline, since both are imposed and carry penalties. Education is learning English, but education is also learning your place. Education might be a discussion with neighbours because of a misdemeanour – it is a telling off, and the offender is given a few books of Mao or Lenin to read. Education might also be a 'struggle session' or something similar with the local committee – 'Change your ways or else', and many books of Mao or Lenin to read. But education also means a pig farm in Inner Mongolia, a farm in Shenyang or Ganzi province – long days slopping the hogs or planting trees, and studying Communist texts at night. In China, the most extreme form of education is prison.

At Lu Shan, a hill station above the Yangtze port of Jiujang, Harry Laughlin pointed to one of the millionaires walking up a hill and said, 'He's captious – that's what we call his type.'

Harry, a millionaire too, sometimes described himself

as an educator. He had taught psychology – never mind his two Mercedes (or Lurabelle's Rolls).

'He's insecure,' Harry said, as we walked along the stony path to the pagoda. 'Notice how he's always alone? He's trying to prove something. He always walks ahead, always apart from the group. See, he wants to show us his ass. Very interesting. He's making a statement there.'

I had thought that the odd-man-out was Mr Clark, because he was almost eighty-two and kept stepping on his camera. Or he would look up and smile and say, 'I lost my pen. I had that pen for years.' He became friendly with Dr Ringrose, and then I decided Dr Ringrose – 'Ring-nose', one of the New York ladies called him – was the odd-man-out. He was a cancer doctor from Calgary, but originally from Leeds. He had some Yorkshire traits – downrightness, unsmiling humour, practicality – but also a sense of grievance. He dressed like a camper. He was a bachelor; he was very intelligent; and he was a pedant. He boasted about his travels and his books. In that grey guest house at Lu Shan he said, 'I have six thousand books. People in Calgary are amazed.'

Lu Shan was a quiet gloomy place, paradise for the Chinese who visit there. It is the opposite of every other Chinese city I had seen. It was cool, not crowded, nor elbow-bumping. The Chinese did not seem to notice Lu Shan's smell or its decrepitude. It was exotic – they made movies there, because the landscape – the piney backdrop, with cliffs and peaks and deep valleys – was the classical Chinese topography. The package tours from Shanghai and Nanjing to Lu Shan cost thirty to forty *yuan*, about a month's wage.

The Chinese went in groups marvelling at the azaleas and dwarf cedars and the lone pines and waterfalls they recognized from scroll paintings. The rhododendrons were tall bushy trees. The architecture was very English-looking – stone bungalows and stone shops, and a large stone church. The Catholic church had been turned into a movie theatre (a bust of Chairman Mao in the foyer) and that month they were showing *She*, a love story. On the hill paths there were little signs carved in Chinese characters in the grey stone. 'Share happiness, share difficulties' – the slogan of a Chinese general in the 1920s. Near a stone seat, the motto: 'Sitting here and dreaming here'.

In the early morning Lu Shan resembled every hill station I had ever seen, from Simla and Fraser's Hill, to the ones above Medan in Sumatra, and Surabaya. The people had rosy cheeks, the pine trees dripped, the stone bungalows were dark and dampstained, and the low cloud and fog settled over the mission steeples and villa roofs until their outlines were faintly pencilled in the mist. The gloom in the place was the same gloom I had noticed in other hill stations, perhaps a result of the fact that such places were entirely a European invention, the architecture English and unmanageable, and the inheritors rather baffled by the layout. The Lu Shan Guest House had English virtues – fine banisters and light fittings and solid walls. But the rooms smelled of damp, the lights did not work, and the whole place had lost its ornaments – no pictures, no plants. The previous occupants had moved out, the new occupants – being poor – could not furnish the house properly.

In Lu Shan I listened to our Comrade Tao question one of the millionaires' wives about life in America.

Mr Tao asked, 'Is rent very high in America?'

'I've never paid rent,' the American lady said.

This surprised Mr Tao. He said, 'What about food? You must spend ten or twenty dollars a week on food.'

'Twenty dollars is nothing,' the lady said.

In China it was almost a month's salary.

'Do you have a bicycle?' the Chinese man asked.

'Yes, I do, but I only use it for fun.'

'A bicycle for fun!' he said. 'What about a car – do you have one?

'Yes.'

'What kind is it?'

This was a difficult question. The lady could not answer. She said, 'Actually, I have four cars.'

Comrade Tao seemed to swallow something very large, and he blinked and squinted at the lady, who had become self-conscious and was saying, 'There's a Chevy convertible, but I can't really use it in bad weather. I usually take one of the smaller ones – they're easier to park, and you save gas. And the others . . .'

Comrade Tao stared.

But the lady had seen her mistake and tactfully changed the subject to azaleas.

Near Lu Shan was a nursery and botanical garden. I asked what effect the Cultural Revolution had had on the operation of the botanical garden and the nursery. The director said, 'All my greenhouses were destroyed for being bourgeois.'

There were faint traces of huge 'big character' slogans on the façade of the Lu Shan Guest House. No one would translate them for me, and two Chinese men denied seeing them.

The millionaires on the Yangtze were always polite, always sociable and always stayed off contentious topics. 'Don't talk to So-and-so about politics,' Jerry McCarthy said. 'No way! Don't mention the Equal Rights Amendment.' Occasionally I heard people issue warnings like this; it meant that a contentious topic had been discovered and was to be avoided in the future. In this way an atmosphere of agreement was maintained.

But when they played games they played to win. I played gin rummy with one of them and he spent the whole time badgering me, mocking me, telling me what I was doing wrong, predicting my discards. He was actually very angry at one point, and after about eight games, when it was clear that I had beaten him, he cursed and stomped away.

The next day he followed me around the deck saying, 'The shill . . . the gin rummy expert . . . the novice,' and he demanded that I play him again.

'This time we'll play for a dollar a point, just to keep up your concentration. What do you say, Paulie-boy? What about it? A rematch! Come on!'

He was not happy until he had beaten me three nights in a row, and then he refused to play me again on the pretext that it was a waste of his time. So I played gin rummy with the ladies from New York, who proved exhausting opponents.

I played Scrabble, and that was worse. I had never played such unenjoyable Scrabble in my life. And the fact was that most of the Scrabble players cheated, or tried to slip non-words by me. One lady insisted that adze was spelled 'adz'. There was no English dictionary on our ship, and she claimed that if there had been she would have been vindicated. Another Scrabble player claimed that 'yo' was a word. When I challenged her, she said, 'Yo-ho-ho!'

They were also full of odd information. The paint on an airplane fuselage weighs between 150 and 400 pounds – there was a fuel economy in flying unpainted planes. I was told that by one of our millionaires while we were touring Nanjing. 'And did you know that Robert Redford is really very short?' a lady said one day. 'No bicycle in China has gears but every one of them has a lock,' a man said. Observant!

I discovered the term for yogurt in Chinese was *suan niu nai*. (Cheese does not exist in China.) I ordered some and was eating it with pleasure, when Doctor Ringrose said, 'We put yogurt on certain forms of skin cancer.'

And they asked questions, sometimes the damnedest

questions. Before we went ashore at Hankow a lady asked the Chinese tour leader, 'What shall I wear?' She meant what style of dress.

At the thermos bottle factory, Mr Clark asked the American guide, 'How many pounds per square inch is the pressure on that glass blowing apparatus?'

At the Wuhan Conservatory, Mr Jones asked, 'What is the name of that instrument?' He was told it was a harp, but he wanted its Chinese name. The musician looked at him and said loudly '*Zhong!*'

People asked how much water flowed through a particular spot on the Yangtze, and what the depth was, and the width, and the population here and there ('Four or five million' was a frequent answer to many different questions). I decided that demanding statistics was a way of getting their money's worth – why else would someone pay $10,000 to sail through China?

At Hubei Medical College Hospital one of the millionaires gazed at an electrical transformer hooked up to some acupuncture needles that were inserted into a patient's wrists.

'How much voltage?' he asked.

He was told.

'Is that a.c. or d.c.?' he asked.

He was told, and satisfied that it was d.c., he walked away.

All over the river people were fishing, some with hooks and lines, others with circular weighted nets, or curtains of nets which they trailed behind their sampans, or the complicated tentlike nets in bamboo frames that Abbé David saw raised and lowered in Shashi. They caught tiny fish – sardine-sized, and they kept even the minnows. More modern methods might have emptied the Yangtze of all its fish, but Comrade Sun had told me that some men still fished with trained cormorants and otters.

The river had widened again: on this stretch of the river I was seldom able to see the far bank, and we sailed to Jiujang in a heated mist, glad for the night at Lu Shan ('The road is very twisty,' Mr Chen said, 'but we have a good driver and he will not go bananas'). In both Jiujang and Lu Shan, people could be seen fighting for cinema tickets. The same films were playing in both places, *The Great Dictator* and *City Lights*, starring China's favourite actor, Cha-Li Zhuo Bi-lin.

On our way to Nanjing, I talked to the *Kun Lun*'s captain. Like Captain Liu of *Number 39*, he had worked his way up to captain, from steward, by on-the-job training, and had never gone to naval college. 'There is no reason for a man to remain a steward his whole life. I tell my men – "Work hard and there will be promotions for you."'

I asked him what the difficulties were in navigating on the Yangtze.

'Two main ones,' he said. 'From December to March, the water is very low and the channel is narrow. This makes things difficult, because there is so much other traffic on the river. The second is the weather. There is fog and mist from October to April, and sometimes it is

impossible to see what lies ahead. Radar is often no help.
To avoid getting into an accident, some nights we anchor
until the weather clears.'

I said that it seemed that very little had changed on the
Yangtze. People fished in the old way; they sailed and
rowed and towed wooden junks; they watered their
fields carrying buckets on yokes; and right back there at
Jiujang, women were washing clothes, clubbing bundles
of laundry and thrashing it in the muddy water. They
crossed the river in rusty ferries and still drowned by the
score when the river was in flood.

The captain reminded me of the Four Modernizations
and said that with the smashing of the Gang of Four,
things would improve. How ironic, I thought: the leader
of the Gang of Four had probably sat in this very cabin;
she was certainly responsible for its décor.

'Before Liberation, this river was different. The

foreigners were very careless. They ran rampant. The Chinese people hated and feared them, because they had a reputation for not stopping for a junk or a sampan, or they might swamp a small boat in their wake. It made them unpopular. The gunboats were the worst of all. The foreigners were disliked for the way they used the river – Japanese, French, Italian, English, American. But things are different now.'

We went ashore at Nanjing. The Gang of Four trial had started. We were encouraged to watch it, by the China Travel Service guides: it reminded me of Hate Week in *1984*, and the defendants looked sick and crazy after four years in prison. I ended up playing gin rummy with Harry Laughlin, who said he was dying to get back to Pasadena.

Above Sun Yat-Sen's mausoleum in Nanjing, there was a slogan which was translated in my guidebook as 'The world belongs to the people'.

I mentioned this to Mr Gregory, one of the Connecticut millionaires. Mr Gregory said President Carter was stupid. Mr Gregory was also an authority on semi-precious stones, and he told me that he had owned more than twenty Cadillacs. He had the security and burglar alarm business and one day he told me, 'I think it's about time the world started to be afraid of America again.' He often said something at dinner and the whole table of ten went silent. Then someone would smile at a big bowl and say, 'Now what do you suppose *that* is?'

'The world belongs to the people,' Mr Gregory said. Then he breathed hard. 'Well, that's not true.'

'Why not?'

'The world belongs to *some* people, but not *the* people.'

He was speaking of the world as it ought to be, not as it was.

'No, sir, not *the* people.'

Later I came across a different translation, without the loaded word 'people'. 'The world belongs to everyone,' it said.

I mentioned this to Mr Gregory.

'That's better,' he said. 'That's true.'

He liked everyone, but he certainly didn't think much of the people.

Slogans were often a problem. At the Xiao Ying Primary School in Nanjing, a slogan which had been painted on a wall at the time of the Cultural Revolution had read, 'Never Forget Class Struggle'. Half of it had been obliterated. It read, 'Never Forget'.

Then there were the Four Modernizations: Defence,

Science and Technology, Industry, and Agriculture. At school, children were taught the Five Loves: Love Work, Love People, Love Neighbours, Love Science, Love Public Property. In the mid-1970s the Eight Antis were to be supported, and it was patriotic and comradely to be Anti-Intellectual, Anti-Western, Anti-Bourgeois, Anti-Capitalist-Roader, Anti-Revisionist, Anti-Traditional, Anti-Confucian, and Anti-Imperialist.

It was important to remember that the Four News were different from the Four Modernizations, and that the Four Olds were especially pernicious. I never discovered what the Four Olds were.

Slogans of an abusive nature had been removed from the building façades in western China, but many of Chairman Mao's picturesque phrases still remained lettered on the walls of certain buildings, and it was one of the pleasures of China to hear these translated by our guides. 'Yes, it says, "Despicable American Imperialists and Their Running Dogs Must Never be Allowed . . ."'

The name of the oldest restaurant in Suchow, The Pine and Crane (perhaps 300 years old?), was thought to be too bourgeois during the Cultural Revolution, so it was changed to The East is Red Restaurant. Recently it has been changed back to The Pine and Crane. Heavenly Park, an ancient garden, was changed to Workers' Park, but it has also reverted to its original name.

Many slogans seemed to me to be defacing public property. In China anyone would write anything anywhere: 'Love Public Property' might be scrawled on a fine building. Slogans were merely a form of public *graffiti*. In the Yangtze Gorges some of the *graffiti* were very old, but I came across more recent stuff. I went to the formal garden in Suchow called The Garden of The Master of Nets. It had been laid out in the year 1140. In The Pavilion of the Accumulated Void (it is a Taoist concept), the rosewood walls are covered with *graffiti* – for example, 'Li Han Ming Came Here on His Travels 1980'.

We were often invited to admire buildings or objects by the Chinese. Look at this Catholic church! they would say. Look at this jade suit made for a nobleman! Look at these tombs! Their explanations were very brief – a date, an anecdote, a name; and then on to the next sight.

But there were always signs near these sights, and I discovered that the signs were usually different from the explanations we received. I asked the Chinese guides to translate these signs. They did so with great reluctance, but the experience was illuminating for me.

Caption under a photograph of a Catholic church in Canton, built in 1861: 'In order to build this church people were forced to move away. The citizens felt very angry. People were not allowed to build residences around this church. No person was allowed to look through the windows of this church.'

Caption under a photograph of a Catholic church in Nanjing, built in the 1850s: 'American imperialism took preaching as its cover. All over China they erected churches like this and carried out destructive activities. In 1853, in Shanghai, the Small Sword Society echoed the Tai-Ping rebels. They occupied Shanghai, country and city. The American missionaries joined up with the

Ching Dynasty troops and attacked the Small Sword Society troops, and the church acted as a stronghold. After the Ching troops lost, the American missionaries escorted them to safety at the American Embassy.'

Sign next to the jade burial suit (Han Dynasty, A.D. 25–220) in the Nanjing Museum: 'The feudal rulers exploited the workers before birth, oppressed the labouring peoples, and even after death wanted to wear the blood and sweat of the labouring peoples, as represented by the jade suit. They planned to preserve their corpses. This reflects the tremendous waste of the feudal rulers and reveals the limitless exploitative nature of the feudal rulers.'

Inscription on the Ming Tombs outside Peking: 'The real landlords of this 40 sq. kms. were the peasants. But after the Emperor selected this site, the imperial troops came in like mad animals. They destroyed the orchards and razed the villages. They used military might to expel the labouring peasants, who had been here for centuries, and they occupied the site.

'The numerous peasant families remembered this with malice. They took everything they owned and left behind their destroyed lives.

'After the tombs were established, this area was labelled "Off-Limits". If one of the Masses came here he was caned 100 strokes; if he grabbed a handful of earth he was executed.

'This is the background of the feudalistic ruling classes' oppression of the peasantry . . .'

These explanations are for the Chinese. Foreigners

were given different explanations, or none at all. At the churches, the jade suit, and the Ming Tombs, there was always a Chinese to say, 'Isn't it pretty?'

At Suchow I took the Shanghai Express, the last part of my sail through China. There were policemen at Suchow station barking orders at the people streaming in. The policemen were rather nasty-looking. I had seen such men be very rough in China, at times manhandling cyclists and pedestrians. Now they were barking orders at the travellers, telling them which platform to go to, how to line up and look sharp.

Within a few minutes we were out of the ancient city of Suchow and had lost sight of the canals and the city moat. We travelled across the vegetable fields of Jiangsu. The last hills I had seen were south of Nanjing. Long ago, this plain through which the Shanghai Express was passing was part of the Pacific Ocean: the Yangtze had extended China's land mass and swelled its estuary into several new provinces, over millions of years.

The soil did not look fertile – Chinese soil seldom did. The gardens were oblongs, stretching to the horizons on both sides of the train. This was Chinese topography, the vegetable plot. When there were hills they had vegetables on them. When there was a riverbank it was a riverbank with vegetables. A valley, a plain, whatever – it always looked the same, slightly exhausted and orderly with cabbages.

Someone said, 'Look, a pig!'

Because there were so few animals to be seen, a pig or a

goat caused great interest, and a dog – those rare crosseyed mongrels – was a sensation. The Chinese did not grow flowers except in pots, in parks and for special occasions. The Chinese were practical, unspiritual, materialistic, baffled and hungry, and these qualities had brought a crudity and a terrible fatigue to their country. In order to stay alive they had to kill the imagination; the result was a vegetable economy and a monochrome culture.

Shanghai was commercial, but the advertising often puzzled me: 'Dragonfly Cotton Shoes! They Are Stylish and Cheap!' 'Rado Watch! Styleproof, Scratchproof, Timeproof!' and 'Aero Tennis Racket – Indeformable!'

I decided to have a look at the Antique Exchange. On the way there I met a Chinese man who had worked for the U.S. Navy during the war. He had a perfect American accent. He summed up for me the years since Liberation: 'The first ten years were bad, the next ten years were okay, but the past ten years have been terrible. I don't know how we got through them. It was the Cultural Revolution. Boy, that was terrible.'

I asked him whether he thought there would be another cultural revolution.

'Sure,' he said.

'Why?'

'Mao said so. Another one. And one after that. Just one after the other.'

The Antique Exchange is where the Chinese sell family treasures to the government, so that they can be resold in the government antique shops and Friendship Stores (which are full of valuable and pretty museum pieces).

On the high stool of a darkened room sits a skinny Chinese man, with yellow protruding teeth and wire-frame glasses. He is sitting cross-legged on the stool, and he wears a skullcap, and he puffs a cigarette by the light of a dim lamp. He points, raises a long fingernail, and beckons a man forward.

The man steps into the light, carrying a canvas bag. He wears a loose army uniform and slippers. He begins to take crockery out of the bag – rice bowls, plates, dishes.

'No, no, no –' The smoker waves this pretty stuff away.

The soldier takes out a stone lion.

'No –'

The soldier puts the lion away, and takes out more rice bowls.

'No –'

The soldier takes out a blue porcelain jar, about ten inches high, luminous and lovely even in this bad light.

The skinny man stops smoking. He sets the jar aside.

There is nothing else. The man shifts on his stool and writes a chit. There is no bargaining: the antique is assigned a price. The soldier puts the rejected stuff into his bag, takes his slip of paper and collects some money.

'They buy things for ten bucks, they sell them for a hundred bucks,' a Chinese man told me in Shanghai. Shanghai was full of English speakers, full of slang from the Second World War.

What interested me was that this smoky seedy interior was a government bureau. But it was the old China. Outside it, a sign in Chinese said: 'Sell Your Old Plates,

Bronzes and Carvings for Cash'. Of course, this is capitalism in the service of the state, buying up heirlooms to sell to tourists, but the old man, the back room, the shelves of cracked porcelain and the dusty bronzes, and the pitiful prices, the pawnshop gloom – it all looked as old as China.

The antique shop prices were very high, but most of the merchandise deserved to be in museums. How long, I wondered, would these treasures be available to tourists?

Not everyone saw these objects as treasures. There was a New York lady, Dorothy Hirshon, who would squint at an item on the shelf and say, 'That's the ugliest thing in China.'

One night after dinner, at about nine o'clock, I went for a walk down a dark street. I had been walking only about ten minutes when I was greeted ('Good evening, sir') by three young men, Comrade Ma, Comrade Lu and Comrade Wee. They wanted to practise their English. I said that I had been reading the supernatural stories of Pu Sung-ling, his *Strange Tales of Liao-chai*. I asked them whether they believed in ghosts. They found this very funny.

'I don't believe in ghosts,' Comrade Ma said.

I asked him why not.

'I never see one.'

I said, 'So there are no ghosts in China?'

'No,' Comrade Lu said.

'What about your ancestors?' I asked.

Comrade Ma said, 'They are under the ground.'

I asked them whether they celebrated the Ching Ming

Festival by exploding firecrackers in the graveyards. They said they didn't celebrate it at all.

'Overseas Chinese do that.'

We were passing a railway embankment where, behind a row of trees, there were young people kissing. They embraced standing up, in the shadowy side of the tree trunks. I called attention to it.

Comrade Ma said, 'Since the Gang of Four were smashed there is now kissing. From 1949 until the Gang of Four there was no kissing. Now there is kissing. Even on television there is kissing.'

'Did the Gang of Four kiss?'

'Oh, yes. But inside their houses!' Comrade Ma said. The others laughed. They regarded Ma as a great wit.

I asked whether they themselves kissed girls.

Comrade Ma said, 'Comrade Liu has a darling. He kisses. I have two darlings. I kiss them.'

I said, 'Indoors or outdoors?'

'Only married people can kiss indoors, in a room. We kiss over there. In the trees. Sometimes in the park. In the park, at night, you can put your hands around the girl – and other places. Ha-ha! Also other things. But it is very stony on the ground – too many rocks!'

'Mister Paul,' Comrade Wee said. 'What is the proper way to kiss?'

He had told me earlier that he was a printer. This inspired me. I said that kissing was like printing. You printed your lips on the girl's lips – not too hard. They laughed and said, yes, that's what they thought it was like.

61

I asked them when they planned to get married. They said when they were about thirty-five or so. They were twenty-six and twenty-seven, and each earned 50 *yuan* ($30) a month.

The trial of the Gang of Four had recently started, so I asked, 'Are the Gang of Four guilty?'

'Oh, yes. Guilty.'

'But not Chairman Mao, eh?' I said. 'Chairman Mao was a great man, right?'

Comrade Ma smiled at me and said, 'Maybe.'

Comrade Wee said, 'Do you think so?'

'I don't know,' I said.

'You are very clever!'

We talked about the Yangtze. The people there, they said, had different clothes and different 'hairs'. This topic provoked Comrade Lu to tell me that his father lived in Surinam – in South America, of all places. But he hated it. 'Too many Negroes.' Hong Kong was better, Lu said.

Comrade Ma told me that he had a bicycle, a TV and a radio. I said that he had everything, apparently.

'No. I want to go to Hong Kong.'

They all agreed: they all wanted to go to Hong Kong. But they had never been outside Shanghai. They lived with their parents, and would go on living with them until they married. I asked whether they regarded themselves as revolutionaries. No, they said, they were workers.

'I don't want to be a revolutionary,' Comrade Ma said.

Had they been in the army?

'There are too many people in the army,' Comrade Lu

said. 'They like the army. It is better than farming. Harvesting rice is hard work. It is easier to be a soldier.'

They were cheery, candid fellows, and we continued walking the dark streets of Shanghai, talking about everything.

What about sports? I asked.

'Table tennis,' Comrade Ma said.

'Badminton,' Comrade Lu said.

'I take' – Comrade Wee glanced nervously at the others – 'I take cold showers.'

In Shanghai, as in other cities in China, the air was bad, it stank, it was dark brown. There were people in the streets, mobs of them, because their rooms were so small and crowded. The streets were free. There is little sign of money, no sign of wealth. Small ugly coins and filthy paper rags are money – it is worthless stuff. The people have clean faces and they observe a kind of ragged order. One can only compare this to the anarchy and distress of India. Here there are scarcely any beggars; there is little apparent violence. Most people are dressed exactly the same. They all wear shoes.

There is a powerful silence in these streets, and the junkyard smell – dust and old rags – is not the smell of death but of illness. Motor traffic would make these cities uninhabitable, but in a crude way the people have made motors unnecessary. The people seldom talk – their silence is the most amazing thing.

For these billion people this is probably the only system that would work. Under capitalism, five percent would be conspicuously rich, and the rest rather poor or very poor, the starving and begging society of China's past. A non-begging society is a good thing – more than that, it is unique. Now, the people ask for nothing. They get very little. If there were disorder here, even a slight amount, I had the impression there would be catastrophe.

Any change in China would be for the worse, which is a pity because it seemed so bad when I sailed through it. Would it always be these people in cheap cotton clothes, walking through the streets, carting the steel rods that are used for these awful buildings, saying nothing? The air pollution gives China the look of existing in a permanent sunset. It worried me that China might never be better than it is now, and that water might always be scarce, clothes always rationed, food never plentiful, houses always tiny, and the hard work never done.